Daddies:

An Endangered Species

Daddies:

An Endangered Species

by
Bill Haltom

GUILD BINDERY PRESS

DADDIES: AN ENDANGERED SPECIES

PUBLISHED IN MEMPHIS, TENNESSEE
BY GUILD BINDERY PRESS
P.O. Box 38099
Germantown, TN 38183

ISBN 1-55793-067-8

Editor and publisher: Randall Bedwell
Senior editor: Palmer Jones
Contributing editor: Robert Kerr
Cover design: Patterson Design Works
Text design: Beverly Cruthirds, Cruthirds Design

Haltom, William H., Jr.
Daddies: An Endangered Species
          p.   cm.

First printing
10 9 8 7 6 5 4 3 2 1

For Reverend William H. Haltom, Sr.

*Daddy, when I grow up,
I want to be just like you.*

Introduction

Bill Haltom is a very funny man. He is also a decent human being. Those two qualities have a lot to do with the fact he is a good daddy and a fine newspaper columnist.

I laughed aloud the first time I read Bill's columns in *The Memphis Daily News*.

I rejoiced when I became an editor and had the opportunity to further the reach of his wit, charm and philosophy.

Bill bristles at these accolades. He considers fatherhood a high calling and the ability to write about it a privilege.

He writes from the heart. His columns are personal and poignant. And funny. Bill makes us feel good. He renews our faith in the family.

And he makes us laugh.

Colleen Conant
Editor
Naples Daily News

Acknowledgements

As a part-time humor columnist, full-time lawyer, and full-time daddy, I need all the help I can get. Fortunately, over the last few years, many wonderful people have encouraged me to write something other than briefs. Specifically, this *Daddies* book would not have been possible without the encouragement of John Hester, Polly Palmer Ward, Nancy and Jack Reese, Nancy and Roy Herron, Mimsy Jones, Stephanie Turnbull, Laurel Campbell, Jack Jones, Jerome Wright, Amanda McGee, Richard McFalls, Charles Brown, Charlotte Durham, Joan Lollar, Paula Casey, Buck Lewis, Dawn LaFon, Ginny LaFon, Suzanne Landers, Palmer Thomason Jones, Bob Troutt, George Whitley, Van Pritchartt, Dan Campbell, Maria Cote, Steve Hart, Suzanne Robertson and Mike Nelson.

Special thanks should also go to my partners at the firm of Thomason and Hendrix for their extraordinary support over the years, even in times when I'm sure my columns embarrassed the members of an otherwise-respected law firm.

I am particularly indebted to the late Lionel Linder, a kind and gentle man who first gave me the opportunity to write for a major daily newspaper.

Special thanks go also to Colleen Conant for giving me the opportunity to write for her wonderful newspaper.

Special thanks also go to my dear friend Joni Prouser for her tireless work on behalf of a computer-illiterate daddy.

And special thanks to my friend Irene Gardner for the cover photo and to my buddy David Jendras of the *ABA Journal* for the illustrations that accompany the text.

Finally, here are a couple of special messages for four wonderful people who provided all the material for this book.

For Will, Ken, and Margaret Grace, I love you, and I'm proud to be your daddy.

And to the love of my life, Claudia Swafford Haltom, thank you for the opportunity to be the father of your children. Thank God they look like you.

Preface

I come from a long line of daddies. My father was a daddy. So were my grandfathers on both sides of the family. In fact, according to my genealogical research, my family has a long history of daddies dating back to my Great-Great-Great-Great-Grandpappy Adam.

Yep, being a daddy is kind of a tradition for the menfolk in my family.

I'm now carrying on the family tradition. I'm the proud father of two handsome sons and a gender-correct baby, who is so beautiful she makes the Gerber baby look downright ugly.

But I have to tell you, I'm worried about the future of daddies. I'm afraid that we old-fashioned daddies are going the way of the dinosaur.

Nearly 25 percent of the children in America are being raised in a daddyless household.

Worse yet, there are a growing number of so-called experts in America who are suggesting that daddies aren't really necessary. Holding up Murphy Brown as the child-rearing prototype of the late 20th century, these experts now tell us that kids don't need daddies. According to these experts, all children really need are "nurturers," since there is no unique contribution that men have to play in raising children. One of these experts was quoted in the Atlanta Journal Constitution as saying, "You should judge the family by the quality of the parenting, not by whether there is a father present."

Indeed, in the New York Public School System, elementary school children were recently reading a book called *Heather has Two Mommies*, a wonderful story about a little girl who is being raised by two women.

Well, call me old fashioned, but the only advantage I can possibly think of for a little girl who is being raised in a household with two mommies and no daddy is that she never has to worry about lowering the toilet seat.

Fortunately, I wasn't raised by two mommies. I was raised by one wonderful mommy and one equally wonderful daddy. Every day of my life, I thank God for that.

The simple truth is that America needs old-fashioned daddies now more then ever.

We need daddies who stick around after conception. How long? Oh, for the rest of their lives.

We need daddies to help deliver their babies.

We need daddies to rock their babies to sleep at night while singing a deep baritone rendition of *Eensy Weensy Spider.*

We need daddies to change diapers, drive carpool and pay for the pediatric orthodontist's Mercedes.

We need daddies to teach their sons how to throw a split-finger fastball or to glide their daughters around the dance floor at the father-daughter dance.

We need daddies on Christmas Eve to help Santa assemble toys that could be put together only by graduates of the Massachusetts Institute of Technology.

We need daddies to finance the family pilgrimage to Walt Disney World.

We need daddies to get the children out of the house on a Sunday afternoon so that Momma can take a well-deserved nap.

We need daddies to take the kids to church or the synagogue and to scout meetings and soccer games.

We need daddies with video cameras filming piano recitals and birthday parties and school pageants.

We need daddies to be male role models for their sons.

We need daddies who think their daughters are perfect, because more often than not, such thinking turns out to be a self-fulfilling prophecy.

We need daddies to help with homework, to attend parent-teacher conferences, to sign report cards and to say to our kids, "I'm proud of you."

We need daddies on graduation day and at weddings and baptisms and Bar Mitzvahs.

We need daddies because, despite what the so-called experts say, men have a unique contribution to play in raising well-adjusted, happy children.

For the past several years, I have shared the trials and

tribulations of fatherhood in a weekly newspaper column. Several of the columns are reprinted in this major work of American literature that you now hold in your hands.

I hope you enjoy the columns. I hope they make you laugh out loud and ask yourself, "When is this hilarious daddy going to write a sequel?"

But I also hope that reading these columns will make you more thankful for old-fashioned daddies who love and care for and shape the lives of their children.

—Bill Haltom

Contents

Daddies: An Endangered Species

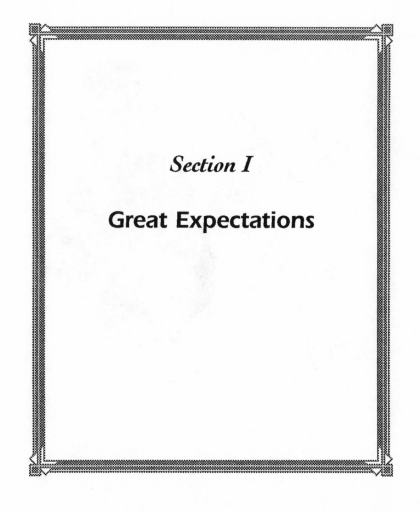

Section I

Great Expectations

Good-Bye Fast Track... Hello, Daddy Track!

If I think hard enough, I can actually remember what life was like before my wife and I went into the baby business.

Yes, it's coming back to me now. Reagan was president (actually he was our official national grandpa), and my wife and I were your typical early 1980s two-career couple. Yuppies in love. It was pretty disgusting.

For the first four years of our marriage, my wife and I rushed through life as if we were the Dallas Cowboys executing the two minute drill.

We should have been the official poster kids for the National Decaffeinated Coffee Counsel.

My wife was your stereotypical, overachieving young lawyer in a hurry. She tried cases, led civic groups, tastefully redecorated an old house, jogged, read books on the *New York Times* best seller list, and accumulated frequent-flyer points.

And on the seventh day, she rested. She did it all. They could have made a Michelob commercial about her.

I worked about 17 hours a day, and considered becoming an investment banker, even though I didn't have the slightest idea what in the heck they do for a living.

My wife and I ate out a lot during those fast-track days of

the early 1980s. We would enjoy romantic candlelight dinners, stare longingly into each other's eyes, and whisper sweet nothings about adjustable-rate mortgages.

Her people would call my people.

We skied.

We ate designer ice cream.

We were skinny.

And then all of that changed. We had a baby.

Of course, we had planned that, too. And we thought we had also planned everything that would happen after the arrival of the little bundle of joy. After natural childbirth and an appropriately long maternity leave, the era of supermom and superdad would begin. Our little baby would have his very own frequent-flyer number and a leather diaper bag.

But a funny thing happened to supermom and superdad on our way to the Land of Quality Time.

To put it bluntly, the little fellow changed our well-ordered lives. And if that wasn't enough, another little person moved into our amazing shrinking house a few years later.

And if that wasn't enough, my wife and I then decided to re-enact the Biblical story of Abraham and Sarah and have a gender-correct baby at about the same time we qualified for membership in the American Association of Retired Persons.

It has been over a decade since my wife and I left the fast track and got on the mommy and daddy track. Over the last several years, my wife and I have changed diapers more often than we have filed briefs.

We have juggled cases, clients, and car-pool schedules.

We have dictated legal memoranda on our pocket dictaphones while rocking a child to sleep. On one occasion, I forgot to turn off my dictaphone, and my secretary ended up typing all the words to the song *Eensy Weensy Spider*.

My wife and I stopped reading books on the *New York Times* best seller list. The last book my wife read was *Pat the Bunny*, and just last night I finished an epic novel called *The Cow Says Moo*, which is soon to be a major motion picture.

We don't travel as much as we used to. When business requires that we travel, we try to fly out early in the morning, get the business done, and fly back in time to be home at night so that we don't miss the next chapter of *Winnie the Pooh and the Honey Tree*.

We don't eat out as much as we did a few years ago. When we do, we tend to go to restaurants that serve meals in brightly colored boxes with pictures of dinosaurs on the side.

No doubt about it, for Ward and June Haltom, life on the fast track is over. But we have no regrets. In too few years, Wally and Beaver and her Royal Highness the Princess will have left the nest and will head off to college to spend our money.

June and I will have plenty of time left to climb all those

career mountains once the days of dinosaurs, Barbie dolls, soccer, and tee-ball games have come to an end.

Besides, I don't want to go back to the fast track. I'm having too much fun. *The Cow Says Moo* is one heck of a book, and nobody, not even Sinatra, can sing *Eensy Weensy Spider* like I can.

The Ultrasound:
Here's Looking At You, Kid

L ast Thursday morning I spent a few minutes watching my third child. That might not sound like something special, but consider this: The kid isn't even born yet.

The stork isn't scheduled to visit our house again until next spring. But thanks to a modern-day medical miracle called ultrasound, my wife and I have already had the opportunity to get a brief glimpse of the little bundle of joy.

A few years ago, there was a television commercial in which a man appeared on the screen and solemnly said, "I'm not a doctor, but I play one on TV." Having stated his impressive medical credentials, the man then went on to tell us what sort of pain reliever we ought to buy.

Well, folks, not only am I not a doctor, but I've never even played one on TV. Therefore, I'll be darned if I can explain to you how this ultrasound business works. All I know is some medical technician put my wife on a table and then proceeded to place on her stomach a little device that was connected by wires to a TV set. My wife looked like a human VCR. I kept half expecting her eyes to start flashing "12:00 . . . 12:00 . . . 12:00."

The technician turned on the TV screen, and faster than you could say "national health care," I saw the black and white image of either precious little Bubba Haltom or precious little Cissy Haltom. We couldn't tell whether the baby was Bubba or Cissy, because unlike most movies these days, the ultrasound did not feature full frontal nudity.

As my wife and I stared in amazement at the screen, the medical technician pointed out the baby's head and also pointed to a little quivering object that was shaking like jello. "That's the baby's heart," explained the technician. She then turned up the soundtrack, and my wife and I were actually able to hear the child's heartbeat. It sounded remarkably like the drum solo in *In A Gadda Da Vida*.

I kept expecting the kid to hold up a sign that read, "Hi, Mom and Dad! Send money!"

My wife and I had a great time watching our unborn child star in his or her own ultrasound TV show. The only disturbing moment came when the technician asked my wife, "Do you feel a twinge on your left side?"

My wife misunderstood. She thought the technician had said, "I see a twin on your left side."

My wife screamed, "Twins?!" She then started to jump up off the examining table so that she could proceed to give me the Lorena Bobbitt Home Vasectomy.

Fortunately, the technician and I were able to calm her down and reassure her that there was only one little bundle of joy appearing on the screen.

Well, folks, I've seen some pretty amazing things in my lifetime. I've seen snow-covered mountain peaks and tropical sunsets. I've seen Baptists dance and dogs catch Frisbees, and I've actually met several honest lawyers. But I'm telling you, I've never seen anything more amazing than the ultrasound image of a child whom I hope to hold in my arms sometime next spring.

Would't It Be Cheaper
Just To Scream Into
My Wife's Belly Button?

My wife lives by the slogan, "When the going gets tough, the tough go shopping!" Measured by this standard, I must admit I am a wimp. I hate shopping. In fact, if I am ever found guilty of committing some hideous crime, the judge will probably sentence me to five years of hard shopping in a suburban mall.

I didn't always feel this way about shopping. I enjoyed shopping many years ago when I saw Ronco company commercials on TV.

Ronco, you will remember, gave the American consumer such outstanding products as the Vegematic ("It slices! It dices!"), the Bamboo Steamer, and the Pocket Fisherman, a little rod and reel that slipped right into daddy's coat pocket. All of these items would be advertised on late-night television with a series of grandiose claims culminating with the words, "And it really, really works!"

The prices for Ronco items would always be something memorable like $9.99 or $7.77. The announcer would enthusiastically say something like, "Yes, millions bought the Ronco

Home Barber Kit for $9.99, but you can have one now for only $8.88!"

When I was a kid, I used to order things from Ronco. In fact, for Christmas in 1962 I ordered my mother a Vegematic. I would like to claim that it "really, really worked," but I remember that I broke it when I tried to dice a grapefruit.

Now I don't claim to be a consumer-affairs reporter, but I have recently come across a product that would be worthy of a Ronco late-night commercial. Believe it or not, there is a product called the "Pregaphone" on the market.

The Pregaphone is a "communications device" that is attached to the abdomen of a pregnant lady. By using the Pregaphone, Mommy and Daddy can talk to their unborn child "in utero."

Developers of the Pregaphone say it serves two purposes. First, it helps parents "bond" with their child as soon as possible.

In case you are unaware, yuppie parents are into "bonding" these days. Bonding has nothing to do with Krazy Glue. It is the term for the emotional attachment between the child and the parents.

Yuppie parents feel it is important to reach out and touch their baby, so to speak, as soon as possible after conception. Many yuppies believe that the fetus can hear and recognize the voices of Mommy and Daddy long before birth.

Second, the Pregaphone helps the parents start educating the child as soon as possible. Here again, the marketers of the Pregaphone have hit a responsive yuppie chord. Yuppies believe that it's never too early to start educating their children.

Consider this: At the moment of conception, your child is only three years and nine months away from his entrance to nursery school. You can't start preparing too soon for this important exam. With the Pregaphone you can start teaching your fetus and give him as much as a nine-month head start over the other children in the neighborhood.

I haven't yet seen a television commercial for the Pregaphone. However, one can just imagine what the Ronco Company would have done with this product. "Yes, the amazing Pregaphone! The gift for the woman who has everything and probably wishes she had a whole lot less! Yes, with the amazing Pregaphone you can talk to little Bubba and Sissy even before they enter the world! Teach them to read, sing, dance. Pipe in classical music. Teach them French, Greek, or Latin. Give them the head start they deserve . . . AND IT REALLY WORKS!"

Well, frankly, I don't intend to buy a Pregaphone if my wife and I ever have another child. I'll just do what I did during our previous pregnancies. I'll save my money and scream into her navel.

Doctor Daddy Delivers

My wife and I are now preparing for a visit from the stork. According to my wife's doctor, some time in the next few weeks the stork is absolutely, positively going to deliver us a package containing our third child.

I'm 43 years old. My wife is 40. We should have our names legally changed to Abraham and Sarah.

As I'm sure your Sunday School teacher has taught you, Abraham and Sarah were that mature couple in Old Testament times whom God blessed with a nursery full of babies at that moment in life when old Abe and Sarah were about to start drawing Social Security. As is written in Genesis, Chapter 17, Verse 16, "And the Lord said to Abraham and Sarah, 'YOU'RE WHAT??!!'"

Like Abe and Sarah, my wife and I are celebrating our entry into middle age by having another baby.

I'm walking proof that the public schools definitely need a sex-education curriculum. I haven't a clue where these babies keep coming from.

My wife recently suggested that I have what she calls a "minor medical procedure." I responded that I did not regard a vasectomy as a minor medical procedure but rather as a major medical procedure that should only be performed at the Mayo Clinic.

My wife then said, "Well, I hear it's just like getting a tooth pulled."

I told her, "Honey, it's not your tooth they pull during that minor medical procedure."

But I assured her that I would have a vasectomy just as soon as Hillary Clinton's health-care bill passes Congress.

In the meantime, my wife and I are getting ready for the big event.

Over the last several days, my wife has been trying to reassemble a crib, a high chair, a playpen, a bassinet, and other baby items that we haven't used since Reagan was in the White House. Frankly, we had stored all these items in the attic to save them for our grandchildren.

Meanwhile, I'm busy brushing up on my medical skills. You see, believe it or not, I'm expected to deliver this baby, just as I delivered our previous little bundles of joy.

A generation ago, daddies weren't even allowed in the hospital delivery room. Ward Cleaver, Ozzie Nelson, Ricky Ricardo, your dad, and my dad all paced around in the father's waiting room at the hospital until a nurse would arrive and announce the birth of the baby. Then the new daddy would shake hands with all the other waiting daddies, pass out cigars, and then head back to the office.

But as any modern generation daddy can tell you, in the 1990s we daddies no longer pace around a waiting room. We are now expected to accompany our wife into the delivery room and actually deliver our own babies.

Well, I'm like Prissy in *Gone With the Wind*. I don't know nothin' about birthing babies. But nevertheless, Doctor Daddy is getting ready for the delivery of Her Royal Highness, my daughter the Princess.

Section II

The Early Years:
Potty Training To The Tune
Of Eensy-Weensy Spider

Potty-Training: The Ultimate Challenge For Daddies

Before Wally and the Beav and the Princess came along, my friends warned me that having a child would dramatically change my life. But, in retrospect, there were two important things they neglected to tell me.

First, they didn't warn me that having three children would really change your life. In fact, the impact of each additional child is equivalent to measuring the magnitude of earthquakes on the Richter Scale. Each additional kid multiplies the household tremors by 10.

Second, my friends did not warn me about the most traumatic aspect of fatherhood: potty-training.

In my 43 years on planet Earth, I have undergone two major surgical procedures. I have listened to speeches by Senator George McGovern and to music by Tony Orlando and Dawn. But I have never gone through anything more agonizing, more painful, and more humiliating than potty-training my children.

Now you would think that in this technological age of satellites, personal computers, and the Ronco bamboo steamer, somebody would have come up with a new way to potty-train a child. There ought to be computer software on the subject.

There ought to be an interactive, instructional video on the topic.

But the painful truth is that in the late 20th century, we still potty-train our children the way we teach medical students to be doctors. That is, we provide hands-on demonstrations for their observations.

Moreover, for reasons that I do not fully understand, women have completely abrogated to men in the 1990s the responsibility of potty-training our children. It makes one wonder who in the world will potty-train Murphy Brown's baby.

Now my daughter is only a few months old. Therefore, I haven't yet begun the task of potty-training her. However, I understand that daughters really don't have to be potty-trained. You just give them a book and a Barbie doll, and they figure it out by themselves.

But I can tell you from personal experience that potty-training little boys requires more than reading materials and lectures. It requires an actual demonstration, by a daddy, accompanied by a description of such concepts as technique, range and accuracy.

Several years ago, I went through what the New England Journal of Medicine has documented as the longest potty-training sessions in the history of urology. Every evening after dinner and before the bedtime story, little Beaver and I would have our potty sessions. I did it so often that even when I went to the john alone at work, I would have to catch myself from describing the action aloud as if I were the Brent Mussburger of the office men's room.

Despite weeks of sessions, my son couldn't quite get the hang of it. We would talk about it before, during, and after the demonstrations, discussing it in minute and humiliating detail.

It got to the point where he himself could call the shots. He knew the process. He knew the technique. But he was your classic consultant. He knew what to do, he just never did it himself.

I started getting desperate. I told my wife, "Honey, if this doesn't change in 18 years, our son will either have to have his own college dorm room, or he'll have to pledge SAE."

But finally, on a glorious autumn night that will live forever in our family history, the little guy quietly went to the bathroom, without a word to Mom or Dad, and as Elvis used to say, he took care of business.

One of my heroes, Erma Bombeck, once said that you forget your anniversary, you forget your spouse's birthday, you forget your own birthday, but you never forget the day your youngest child goes to the potty all by him or herself. Amen, Sister Erma! No truer words were ever spoken.

When my wife and I discovered the evidence that little Beaver had gone to the bathroom by himself, we went absolutely wild. We called in neighbors, family and friends to witness the evidence. We got out the video camera and filmed it. We bragged on him in front of his big brother. We sang songs in his honor. We gave him high-fives. We carried him off the field, and then we shook down the goal posts!

I'm proud of the little fella. And at the risk of sounding immodest, I'm proud of myself, for having successfully potty-trained two little boys. But in the words of the great French philosopher Maurice Chevalier, thank heaven for little girls. Not only do little girls grow bigger every day, but they potty-train themselves.

Potty-Training: The Sequel

I have some really good news for my fellow daddies who have small children. America's toy manufacturers are now marketing several toys that can help us potty-train the kids.

For example, one of the most popular dolls during the past Christmas season was Magic Potty Baby, a doll manufactured by the Tyco Toy Company.

For many years, toy companies have manufactured dolls that wet their pants. However, Magic Potty Baby does not wet her pants. You give Magic Potty Baby her bottle, place her on her very own magic potty, and then, right before your very eyes, Magic Potty Baby takes care of business.

Similarly, the Cabbage Patch Toy Company is now manufacturing the Cabbage Patch Potty-Training Doll. Like Magic Potty Baby, the Cabbage Patch doll does "number one" (to use a medical term) in her very own Cabbage Patch toilet.

But in my unbiased opinion as a daddy consumer-affairs reporter, the very best potty-training toy available is something called Tinkle Time Targets.

I recently read about Tinkle Time Targets in a catalog featuring "educational toys."

According to the catalog, Tinkle Time Targets is a "fun way to motivate children to use the toilet properly—and to encourage boys to aim more carefully."

Each Tinkle Time Target package contains 45 flushable targets, each about one inch in diameter, decorated with animals in a variety of colors. The "non-staining" targets will float in your toilet bowl until hit directly by a well-aimed shot from a little boy.

Yes, kids, it's ready, aim, and fire with Tinkle Time Targets!

So help me, the toy company that manufactures Tinkle Time Targets advertises that its potty-training toys will "help children and their parents come to grips with the trials and tribulations of potty-training."

Yes, and we daddies will no doubt be flushed with pride when we see our toddlers score a direct hit on a Tinkle Time Target.

To my knowledge, Tinkle Time Targets is the only potty-training toy that has been endorsed by the National Rifle Association.

Next Christmas season, you might want to buy Tinkle Time Targets as a Christmas gift. As far as I'm concerned, Tinkle Time Targets would be the perfect Christmas gift for any daddy who has little boys who are not yet potty-trained.

With the help of Tinkle Time Targets, Daddy might not have to change a single diaper during the entire Christmas season.

You might say, I'm dreaming of a wiped Christmas.

Six Months Ago I Couldn't Spell Paleontologist And Now My Son Are One

L ife is full of surprises, especially when you are a daddy. The other evening at dinner my 3-year old son startled me by calmly making the following announcement: "Daddy, when I grow up I'm going to be a paleontologist."

I started to say, "Too late, kid, you have already been baptized an Episcopalian."

But then I came to an embarrassing realization. I hadn't the slightest idea what a paleontologist was.

Now, when I had my daddy training a few years back at the Famous Daddies School (not affiliated with the Columbia School of Broadcasting), one of the things they taught us was, "Never let your 3-year-old know he is smarter than his daddy."

So I remained calm, and I requested a brief private consultation in the kitchen with the boy's mother.

"June," I said, "would you please tell old Ward here what in the Sam Hill Wally is talking about."

Adjusting her pearls, my wife responded in her best condescending voice, "Oh, you know, dear, a paleontologist is one who studies fossils and dinosaurs."

Oh. Well, of course. June and I returned to the dining room and recommenced the sparkling dinnertime conversation.

"So, son," I began, "You like dinosaurs."

"Yes," said Wally.

"Well, that's great son. You know, I like dinosaurs, too," I said.

"Really, Daddy? Well, what is your favorite kind of dinosaur?"

Wally was calling the old man's bluff. I started to say, "Well, I always liked the little one on The Flintstones." But somehow I knew this response would not satisfy America's youngest paleontologist.

And so, like a bad law professor, I resorted to the Socratic method, answering a question with a question: "Well, son, why don't you tell me your favorite dinosaur?"

"A diplodocus," Wally replied without hesitation.

Diplodocus? Wasn't he that little Greek fellow the Democrats nominated for President a few years back?

"Do you like diplodocus?" Wally asked.

"Well, I would have liked him a lot more if he hadn't let Willie Horton out of prison on weekends," I replied.

June, Wally and Baby Beaver all stared at me.

I struggled through the rest of dinner like Richard Nixon at one of his last presidential press conferences. I tried to deflect questions concerning the stegosaurus, the pterodactyl and the triceratops. To me, it sounded like Wally was reciting the starting lineup of the Notre Dame football team.

No doubt about it, a wave of dinosaurmania has hit our household. It all started earlier this year when the local museum had its dinosaur exhibit. Wally visited the exhibit eight times. I took him, his mother took him, his grandfather took him, his godmother took him, his playschool class went, and on one occasion, he hijacked a babysitter and demanded that she take him.

Since the museum dinosaur exhibit, Wally's appetite for paleontology has been insatiable. He wants plastic dinosaurs, stuffed dinosaurs, dinosaur books, dinosaur videos, dinosaur food, (they make Spaghetti-O's shaped like dinosaurs), and he even insists on a dinosaur wardrobe. He wants all of his clothes to be decorated with dinosaurs, just as preppies once insisted that their clothes be covered with alligators.

I am not sure I understand this obsession with a bunch of big lizards that died over 100 million years ago. But I guess I really ought to be proud. Six months ago I couldn't spell "paleontologist" and now, as they say, my son "are one."

Blaming Captain Kangaroo

When I was a child, one of my heroes was Captain Kangaroo. As a pre-schooler growing up in the 1950s, I began each day watching the Captain Kangaroo TV show. Dressed in my pajamas and my Davy Crockett coonskin cap, I would sit in front of the TV set and watch the adventures of Captain Kangaroo and his co-stars, Mr. Greenjeans, Mr. Moose, Grandfather Clock, Bunny Rabbit, and Dancing Bear.

I have fond memories of Captain Kangaroo. Every morning on his TV show, he read me stories or showed me farm animals or talked to me about brushing my teeth and minding my parents.

Captain Kangaroo seemed to personify family values. Therefore, I always thought that he was a positive role model for me during my childhood. But according to an executive of the Motion Picture Association of America, I've been wrong about Captain Kangaroo all these years. You see, it turns out that Captain Kangaroo's TV show was a dangerous subversive program that helped spawn the sexual revolution, riots, and a general breakdown in law and order.

The painful truth about Captain Kangaroo came out in a letter that was written by Mr. Van Stevenson, Vice President and lobbyist for the Motion Picture Association of America. Stevenson wrote the letter to a California state senator who had drafted a resolution criticizing the entertainment industry for airing violent children's programs. Mr. Stevenson stated, "There is no credible scientific evidence or statistical data to suggest that if depictions of sex and violence are exiled from movie and television screens that the incidents of real-life teenage violence, pregnancy, and AIDS cases will diminish. In fact, the opposite may be true. The first generation of children television viewers that grew up in the 1950s with a healthy dose of family values of 'Captain Kangaroo,' 'Father Knows Best,' 'The Donna Reed Show,' and 'Ozzie and Harriet' is the same generation that caused the sexual revolution of the late 1960s and early 1970s as well as engaged in the enormous civil unrest and rioting on college campuses during the same time."

That's right, folks. Captain Kangaroo, along with his co-conspirators Ozzie and Harriet, may well have caused the sexual revolution, the break-up of the American family, and the general decline of law and order in our society.

Little did I realize that when Mr. Moose dropped ping pong balls on Captain Kangaroo's head, the Captain was cleverly encouraging four-year old little Billy Haltom to some day engage in acts of civil disobedience. Frankly, I'm surprised that Captain Kangaroo and Mr. Greenjeans were never summoned to testify before the House Unamerican Activities Committee.

If the late Senator Joseph McCarthy had only known what the Captain was really up to, he would have re-named him "Captain Communist."

27

This disturbing news about Captain Kangaroo is, however, good news for executives of the motion picture, music, and television industries. Now whenever Senator Bob Dole or Tipper Gore chastises the entertainment industry for violent and sexually explicit entertainment, these executives can respond, "Don't blame us! Captain Kangaroo started all this!"

Now that we have finally learned the truth about Captain Kangaroo, perhaps it's time we investigate other children's TV stars of the 1950s. Perhaps they too are responsible for everything that's gone wrong in America in recent years.

Perhaps Howdy Doody is responsible for the federal deficit. Perhaps Soupy Sales is responsible for the violence in our society. After all, he was always encouraging the children of America to throw pies at one another.

Now that I think about it, Roadrunner was a subversive revolutionary. He was always dropping an anvil on top of poor Wile E. Coyote, or forcing Wile E. Coyote to run off the side of a cliff.

Little did I realize what a terrible impact Roadrunner had on me as a child. To this day, I often feel this unexplainable urge to drop an anvil on somebody's head.

Frankly, I think the news about Captain Kangaroo has come just in time. We Baby Boomers who now have children of our own can take a long, hard look at what our kids are watching on TV.

For example, now that I know the truth about Captain Kangaroo, I will never again allow my little girl to watch that dangerous subversive, Barney the Dinosaur.

Section III

Where Are Ward And The Aqua Velva Man Now That We Really Need Them?

The Demise Of Male Role Models, Or Where Is The Aqua Velva Man Now That We Really Need Him?

Perhaps the most important reason we need old-fashioned daddies is to provide male role models for our little boys.

I'm a lifelong member of the male gender, and proud of it. Those rumors about my previous career on the women's professional tennis circuit are completely untrue.

No, I haven't participated in one of those "male bonding" retreats where guys sit out in the woods together and celebrate manhood by beating drums. Nevertheless, I'm proud to be a man and to engage in such manly activities as sitting in my lounge chair at night and watching ESPN's celebrity mudwrestling.

But frankly, I'm concerned about the future of my gender. These are tough times for us menfolk. On college campuses, politically correct professors are rewriting the history books so that we men get the blame for everything from pollution to wars to ring around the collar.

You say your grade-school teacher taught that Christopher Columbus discovered America? Well, forget it, kids. Old Chris was just a typical male driver who got hopelessly lost while on a business trip. If Queen Isabella wanted the job done right, she should have taken charge of the expedition herself.

Do you still really believe that nonsense about America's founding fathers being noble and enlightened men who gave us the Declaration of Independence and the Bill of Rights? Boy, are you naive! They were a bunch of sexist pigs who owned slaves and made Betsy Ross sew flags for less than the minimum wage.

In the face of this revisionist attack on my gender, I am concerned about who are the male role models for the little boys now growing up in America.

When I was a child, America had three basic male role models: John Wayne, Clark Gable, and the Marlboro Man. These were strong, tough, self-assured men who rode horses, smoked cigarettes, drank whiskey, ate red meat and never worried about their cholesterol.

Did you ever see John Wayne sitting on horseback eating an oat-bran muffin? Of course not.

The Duke, Rhett Butler, and the Marlboro Man are all gone now. And what do we have in their place? Well, now we have new "sensitive males," such as Alan Alda, Phil Donahue, and the Energizer Rabbit.

In fact, one can make the argument that the only real men we have left in America today are General Normal Schwartzkopf and Nancy Reagan.

Remember the Aqua Velva Man? Now there was another great male role model. The Aqua Velva Man stated a plain and simple truth: A man wants to smell like a man.

That'll preach. Won't it? A man wants to smell like a man!

Well, the Aqua Velva Man is gone now. And what do we have in his place? Calvin Klein—a man who's obsessed with something and I'm not quite sure what it is.

Remember the Brylcreme Man? A little dab would do him, and "the gals" would love to run their fingers through his hair. Nowadays, we men are supposed to dab our hair with something called "mousse," or maybe it's a squirrel.

As a result of these changes, a whole generation of men is now experiencing an identity crisis.

The problem is that we males no longer have a clear vision of what a "real man" is. We've been told that real men don't eat quiche. But what do real men do?

Is a fellow a "real man" if he goes through life constantly reassuring everyone (most of all, himself) that he is not a wimp? Is a fellow a "real man" when he blames everyone but himself for whatever is going wrong? Whatever happened to such manly virtues as sacrifice and responsibility? Did they ride off into the sunset with Duke Wayne?

I don't know. I'm hopelessly confused, and I'm not getting any answers from all those sensitive males who wring their hands and seem to apologize for being gender-incorrect.

Where are Clark Gable and the Aqua Velva man now that I really need them?

Father No Longer Knows Best

A few years ago, Vice President Dan "Mr. Potato Head" Quayle set off a national debate when he criticized the popular television program, *Murphy Brown*. Vice President Danny apparently watches a lot of television, and he got upset over a recent episode in which Murphy had a baby without having a husband to help take care of the baby on future episodes.

Vice President Danny's comments about Murphy Brown were ridiculed by newspaper columnists, politicians, and late-night comedians. Even Johnny Carson devoted part of his "farewell address" to a few parting jokes about Danny Quayle.

But I believe that once again, Vice President Danny was misunderstood. He wasn't calling Murphy a tramp.

Rather, the vice president was simply bemoaning one of the tragedies of our times—the demise of TV daddies.

I know how the vice president feels. Like Danny, I grew up watching TV in the '50s and '60s. It was a golden era for TV daddies. In fact, all of the heroes on TV in the 1950s were either daddies or cowboys.

Daddies were revered figures on TV during the Eisenhower administration. The titles of the shows said it all— *Father Knows Best, Make Room For Daddy, My Mother The Car* ... (Well, o.k., two out of three ain't bad.)

To really understand Vice President Danny's point, just ask yourself this question: What did Beaver Cleaver, Ricky Nelson, Pebbles Flintstone, BamBam Rubble, Opie, Little Ricky, all three sons, and the entire Brady Bunch have in common? They all had outstanding daddies!

The TV daddies of the '50s and '60s were hard-working men who personified the work ethic. Ward Cleaver, Fred Flintstone, Rob Petrie, and Robert Young (who later became Dr. Marcus Welby) all went to the office every day and worked hard to bring home the bacon for June, Wilma, Laura and the kids.

The TV daddies of the '50s and '60s were wise men who were respected by their children.

Moreover, the TV daddies of the '50s and '60s were devoted family men. Ward Cleaver never went through a mid-life crisis and decided to trade in June for a "trophy wife." Ricky Ricardo never ran off with Ethel Mertz.

But in the 1990s the daddies we see on TV are portrayed as dumber than a bucket of rocks. I'm convinced that if they made a sequel to *Father Knows Best*, it would be entitled *Father Doesn't Know Jack.*

We've replaced Robert Young and Ward Cleaver with Homer Simpson and Al Bundy.

So I don't blame Danny Quayle for being upset about Murphy Brown. Little Murphy Jr. needs a daddy who will sing *Baba-Loo* for him just like Lucy's husband did for Little Ricky.

But I do think the vice president overlooked something when he criticized Murphy Brown for glorifying single parents. Sheriff Andy Taylor was a single parent, and Opie turned out all right. And now that I think about it, Fred McMurray was a single parent, and all three of his sons turned out to be splendid.

Of course, Andy had Aunt Bea to help raise Opie, and Fred had Uncle Charlie to cook for Rob, Chip and Ernie.

Maybe Danny Quayle will feel better if Aunt Bea or Uncle Charlie appears in a future episode to help Murphy take care of her baby.

Would Ward Cleaver Wear An Earring? Would June Wear A Tattoo?

I'm so old I can remember when it was women who wore earrings and men who wore tattoos. But in this progressive decade of the 1990s, increasing numbers of men are having their ears pierced while women are having their forearms and their rear-ends permanently embroidered with colorful butterflies.

When I was a kid, only one man in America wore an earring. He was Mr. Clean, the bald-headed guy on the cleanser commercials on TV. He looked pretty goofy wearing one earring. But he could get rid of dirt and grime and grease in just a minute and clean our whole house and everything that was in it.

Mr. Clean was the only guy in America who could get away with wearing an earring. I guarantee you that had my father ever come home wearing an earring, my mother would have pierced both his ears and his skull with a rolling pin.

Of course, I can't even imagine what Daddy would have done if Mamma had gone to a tattoo parlor and come home with her arms decorated as if she were Popeye the Sailor Person.

When I was a kid, the only woman I ever saw who wore a tattoo was Lydia the Tattooed Lady. She was the star of a carnival that came to my hometown in 1959.

But these days, Lydia the Tattooed Lady would hardly stand out at the Junior League meeting.

Last March, I took my kids to the beach at approximately the same time that half the college students of America were in Florida for spring break. Having observed the next generation of Americans in their bathing suits, I can tell you the future of America is (there is no other word for this) ugly.

These days your typical college coeds and college men look like participants in a Dennis Rodman look-alike contest.

Worse yet, millions of our children are not only having their ears pierced, but they are drilling holes in other parts of their bodies as well.

During my family's recent trip to the beach, I noticed an alarming number of young people who had their belly buttons pierced so that they had rings sticking through their navels, causing their stomachs to resemble the front doors of their parents' home.

Well, call me old-fashioned, but I think it's time we daddies speak out against the tattoo and body-piercing fads before it's too late.

You see, one of these days, your typical American coed is going to decide that that butterfly on her rear-end isn't that attractive after all. And Joe Cool, big man on campus, will grow tired of having a body with so many pierced holes in it that he resembles a giant piece of Swiss cheese.

How do I know this? Simple. Back around 1980 I got a short haircut.

You see, tattoos and earrings are to the current generation of young people what long hair was to my generation. From approximately 1968 to 1980, my ears were not pierced, but they did disappear. In fact, during the polyester decade of the 1970s, virtually no man in America had ears. The male ears of America were covered by hair, as I and virtually every member of my generation tried to look like Paul McCartney. Unfortunately, most of us ended up looking like Sonny Bono.

My ears reappeared in the early 1980s as my hair got greyer and shorter. However, all that took was one quick trip to the barbershop. Scraping off all those tattoos and plugging up all those pierced body parts will be a lot more complicated and a lot more expensive.

I say we daddies need to speak up now before our kids start drilling holes in their belly buttons.

We Daddies Are Still In Control, But Only Remotely

In the decade of the '90s, women are seizing power in all institutions of American society.

In politics women have recently won United States Senate seats in California and Illinois, as well as many other Congressional seats across the country. That's fine with me, since it is a proven fact that in most households, it is the wife who balances the checkbook.

In the private sector, women are also taking charge. Women are now running America's corporations, trying lawsuits, broadcasting sports events, getting ulcers, and having heart attacks just like we menfolk have for years.

In short, Andy and Opie and Ward and Wally and Beaver and the rest of us real men are having to adjust to the fact that Aunt Bea, June, Hillary Clinton, Barbara Bush, Nancy Reagan, and her astrologer are now running the country.

But despite these advances by women, we men still control the single most important source of power in most American homes. Yes, we men still hold our powerful masculine hands on the TV remote control.

According to a survey published in a recent issue of *TV Guide*, men are twice as likely as women to hold the remote control in America's households. In 41 percent of American homes, the daddy sits on his lounge-chair throne and exercises exclusive control over the zapper.

In only 19 percent of American homes does Queen Mother exercise exclusive control of the zapper.

In some 27 percent of American homes, the husband and wife have joint custody of the zapper.

This survey raises a provocative sociological question: Why is it that we men are willing to give up political and financial power to women, but steadfastly refuse to turn over to women a small instrument that would allow them to change the channel from Monday Night Football to Murphy Brown?

The answer, of course, is that the fundamental genetic difference between men and women is that we men have the attention span of a flea. For example, when my wife watches television, she has this annoying habit of watching one program at a time. Moreover, she insists on watching one program from the beginning to its conclusion. For example, she spent the entire year of 1983 watching the mini-series, *Winds of War*.

On the other hand, when I watch television, I view as many as 147 programs on a single evening. I watch some of these programs for as long as three or four seconds at a time. I just sit in my lounge chair, aim that zapper at the screen, and push the zapper button every few seconds as if I were Marshall Dillon shooting bad guys.

I have no interest whatsoever in watching an entire program. I just want to surf across the cable waves and get an occasional glimpse of Pat Robertson, the Atlanta Braves, Larry King, Ross Perot, Harry Carey, Bart Simpson and Lassie.

While I'm no Alan Alda, I am a pretty open-minded guy. I'd be more than happy to have a woman president, nine women on the Supreme Court, and a United States Congress that looks like a Junior League convention. But in the words of a former male President, let me make one thing perfectly clear: I'll give up control of my TV when they pry my cold dead fingers off the zapper!

Section IV

Are We There Yet, Daddy?

A Daddy's Pilgrimage To Disney World (Or It's A Small Bank Account You Have After All)

ORLANDO—During my lifetime, I have visited most of the great tourist attractions of the world. I have been to Rock City and seen seven states from high atop Lookout Mountain. I've played some of the most treacherous Goofy Golf courses in Panama City. I've been to the Jungle Room at Graceland for several safaris.

But now, I've seen it all. I'm at Disney World.

I did not come here by choice. Federal law now requires daddies to bring their children here at least once every five years. It's right there on the income tax forms at Question 6A:
"Have you taken your dependents to Disney World this year?"

So on the advice of my accountant, Ernest N. Whiney, I have taken June, Wally, and the Beav on a family pilgrimage.

Disney World consists of three major attractions. The first is called The Magic Kingdom. It is a huge amusement park built in honor of a giant rodent. It is the only place on earth where you can see a robot that looks like Millard Fillmore, or hear bears who can sing like Porter Wagoner.

The second attraction is EPCOT, which is an acronym meaning Everyone's Paycheck Cleaned Out Thoroughly. EPCOT is a sort of combination futuristic fun park and high-tech world's fair. Corporate America is highly visibly in EPCOT. You can watch shows sponsored by General Electric or ride amusement rides sponsored by AT&T. Our favorite part of EPCOT was the Exxon ride. Wally and the Beav and I rode miniature tankers that actually collided, causing a simulated environmental disaster at the Alaskan Pavilion.

The third and newest part of Disney World is the MGM Studio Theme Park. Here you can see how Hollywood (or Orlando) makes outstanding motion pictures such as *When Harry and Sally Met Rambo II and Rocky VI*.

For those daddies who have not yet made a pilgrimage to Disney World (and you better make your travel reservations soon, before you're indicted by the Grand Jury), let me give you two words of warning. First, be prepared to spend your life's savings and then some. Disney World is so expensive that only defense contractors can afford to bring their families here without engaging in deficit spending to rival the Federal government.

Second, be prepared to stand in line for hours, perhaps even days, to get on the really good rides such as the highly-popular It's a Small Bank Account You Have After All.

But despite the cost and the long lines, by all means take out a second mortgage on your house, pack up the kids in the minivan and head for Orlando.

Besides, daddies, you really have no choice but to make the trip. After all, it's the law.

Driving Daddy To The Brink

SOMEWHERE ON THE REDNECK RIVIERA—My family and I are now camped out at a deluxe Motel 6 at a beachside resort on the Gulf of Mexico. Yes, it's that time of year again when middle-class American families take part in that great tradition, The Summer Vacation in Florida.

Each August, thousands of American families escape the heat and humidity of mid-America to journey to Florida, where the daily high temperature is 97 degrees, the humidity is 90 percent, and the heat index is approximately the same as Wade Boggs' lifetime batting average. Next February, these same families will escape the ice and snow of mid-America by taking ski trips to Colorado where the wind-chill factor will be 30 below zero.

The summer vacation in Florida is quite an adventure for us daddies. The excitement begins with a 15-hour ride to Florida through scenic Mississippi. In December, for a daddy, the three most terrifying words in the English language are, "Some assembly required." But in August, the five most exasperating words in the English language are, "Are we there yet, Daddy?"

For 15 mind-boggling hours, Daddy-the-Minivan-Driver hears an endless chorus of, "Are we there yet, Daddy?" Daddy must greet each chorus by calmly responding, "No, kids. We have at least 10 more hours of driving before we get to see Shamu-the-Killer-Whale perform at Sea World." Daddy-the-Minivan-Driver must have the patience of Job, the diplomacy skills of Henry Kissinger, and the driving abilities of Richard Petty.

Once you arrive in Florida, there is no shortage of family entertainment. Among the attractions at the Redneck Riviera are Goofy Golf courses, water slides, Go-Kart race tracks (for Daddies who want to do just a little more driving), a wax museum, and something called Gatorama, where a fellow dressed like Marlin Perkins wrestles alligators. Oh, and by the way, there is also a beach that runs alongside the Gulf of Mexico, although the waves in the Gulf pale in comparison to those you can find at the Surf-A-Rama Water Theme Park.

But despite the 15-hour drive and the endless hours of Goofy Golf, a summer vacation in Florida has one benefit for a daddy.

It makes him actually look forward to the peace and quiet he will experience in a couple of weeks when the kids are back in school and he is off the highway and back in his office.

Disney World Revisited

ORLANDO—For the second time in three years, I'm on a Daddy's Pilgrimage to Disney World. Once again, I did not come here by choice. I was taken hostage and brought here by two little terrorists who also happen to be my sons.

It all started when my wife recently announced that she needed to attend a seminar in Orlando and that maybe the boys and I would like to accompany her, at my expense. Faster than you could say Donald Duck, my boys had packed our bags and I was being dragged kicking and screaming to the airport.

For the past three days, the boys and I have been touring the Magic Kingdom while Mommy attends her legal seminar. Mommy, like Hillary Clinton, is a lawyer. However, unlike Hillary, Mommy is pro-choice on the issue of women baking cookies.

After spending three full days of quantity time with my boys and Mickey Mouse, I'm exhausted. That's because Disney World presents the ultimate challenge for daddies, financially, emotionally, and physically.

Financially, the bottom line is that unless you are H. Ross Perot, you really can't afford to bring your family to Disney World. The only way a normal middle-class daddy like me can pay for a trip to Disney World is to refinance his house. If a daddy takes out second and third mortgages on his home, a family of four may be able to visit Disney World, so long as family members agree not to buy any souvenirs.

Emotionally, a trip to Disney World can push a daddy to the verge of a nervous breakdown. For the past three days, I have marched relentlessly through the Great Mouse's Magic Kingdom while two little boys have constantly pulled my arms in opposite directions. Consequently, my arms have been lengthened, my back is bent, and I now have the posture of a gorilla who needs a really good chiropractor. I have endured 72 consecutive hours of whining from little boys demanding that I take them on such exciting rides as Space Mountain, the Teenage Mutant Ninja Turtle Sewer Ride, and the highly-popular Daddy Financial Roller Coaster Ride.

The boys and I have also attended Disney World shows such as the Country Bear Jamboree, a musical revue featuring mechanical robot bears who sing like George Jones and Tammy Wynette.

We also visited the Disney World Hall of Presidents. This is a patriotic show starring (so help me), robots who look like the Presidents of the United States. While the Disney sound system plays *Hail to the Chief*, each robot president bows to the audience.

The feature star in the Hall of Presidents is (again, so help me) a robot Bill Clinton. He looks, talks and acts just like the real Bill Clinton. There was even a robot Hillary standing behind him, telling him what to say.

The highlight of the Disney Hall of Presidents Show came when the Robot Bill Clinton made a short speech. That's when the boys and I knew it was a robot. The real Bill Clinton could never give a short speech.

Physically, a daddy's pilgrimage to Disney World is strikingly similar to running the Boston Marathon, only it lasts a lot longer and the hills are steeper. The problem is that in order to get on board the rides or see the shows at Disney World, one must stand in lines longer and more crowded than the New Jersey Turnpike. For example, the boys and I stood in line for 45 minutes in order to get on board a submarine ride called "Twenty Thousand Leagues Under the Sea."They should rename it "Twenty Thousand People Standing in Line."

Well, with all due respect to Mickey, Minnie, Donald, and Hillary, I'll be glad when my wife's seminar is over and I am released from Disney World on good behavior.

I'll be so happy to get back home, I'll even bake some cookies for the boys.

Section V

If You Want Your Kids To Learn Something, Send Them To Vacation Bible School

The Benefits Of A
Baptist Education

During the past week, my boys have been attending Vacation Bible School. Early each morning a Baptist minivan has pulled up in front of our house and whisked little Wally and Beaver Haltom off to a nearby church for a busy morning of Bible lessons, gospel sing-alongs, and arts and crafts in which offering plates are constructed out of popsicle sticks.

As a Baptist P.K. (Preacher's Kid), I am an "old grad" of Vacation Bible School. From 1955 to 1964, I spent at least two weeks each summer attending Vacation Bible School. Consequently, I memorized so many scripture verses and built so many offering plates that I deserve a Vacation Bible School Ph.D., a Doctorate of Popsicle-Stick Theology.

The church that my family and I now attend is so progressive that it doesn't have a Vacation Bible School. But there's no reason to despair if you want to get the kids out of the house this summer for a little theological training. Behold, I bring you good tidings of great joy. If you just pick up the phone and call your neighborhood Baptist church, a Sunday school teacher will come, get your children, and take them to Vacation Bible School in 30 minutes or less, which is a better deal than you'll get from any pizza company.

I am delighted that my boys have been attending Vacation Bible School. That's because I want little Wally and the Beav to have the benefit of a good Baptist education.

In recent years, Baptists have been getting some really bad press. This may have something to do with the fact that at their annual conventions, Baptists often cheer Ollie North and boo women preachers. This might give one the false impression that your typical Baptist is someone who would support selling arms to the Ayatollah, but would oppose contributing to the work of Mother Teresa.

But I don't think that's a fair conclusion. Moreover, our children could learn a lot from the Baptists. That's because there are at least two areas in which Baptists have more expertise than anybody in the whole world.

The first is transportation. Baptists know how to move people, whether they are little children attending Vacation Bible School or senior citizens being bussed to Billy Graham Crusades in huge football stadiums. In fact, very few people know this, but the late Walt Disney hired Baptist Sunday school teachers to design the transportation system for Disney World.

The second area where Baptists have particular expertise is fund-raising. I am convinced that if the President really wants to get control of the federal deficit, he should appoint a Baptist preacher to be Secretary of the Treasury.

This is perhaps best illustrated by a story a preacher told me long ago. A busload of Baptists was on an outing and, unfortunately, the bus went over a ravine and all aboard perished. Of course, within the twinkling of an eye, the bus pulled up to the Pearly Gates where the Baptists were met by St. Peter.

Unfortunately, for St. Peter, the timing couldn't have been worse. Heaven was full, and it would be at least two weeks before celestial construction workers had finished building heaven's newest wing to accommodate more souls.

Thinking fast, St. Peter called Satan and made arrangements for the Baptists to spend a couple of weeks in Hell while their new heavenly accommodations were being completed.

A couple of days later St. Peter's phone rang. It was Satan. He said, "Pete, you've got to get these Baptists out of here!"

"What's the problem?" asked Pete.

Satan replied, "These Baptists haven't even been here a week, and they've already raised enough money to air condition this place!"

Well, that's precisely the sort of Baptist know-how that could enable our children to turn this country around. Let's face it. The Japanese will never be able to compete with millions of graduates of Vacation Bible School.

School Kids Haven't Got A Prayer

The U.S. Supreme Court recently issued the latest in its series of "thou shalt not pray" commandments to America's schoolchildren. The nation's highest court, which banned prayer in the classroom some 30 years ago, now says that the U.S. Constitution forbids prayer at public-school commencement exercises.

In other words, in the future, it will be unlawful for a minister, priest or rabbi to stand up at the conclusion of a public high-school graduation ceremony and ask God's blessings on the graduates. From now on, the principal will just hand out the diplomas and then say, "Well, good luck, kids. You're on your own now. Have a nice day."

I imagine some overly religious school administrator or principal will try to sneak a prayer in at a graduation ceremony. But faster than you can say "Amen," the American Civil Liberties Union will hire some fancy-pants lawyer who will serve the principal with an injunction.

I attended public schools from the first grade through law school, and I must confess I prayed a lot during my school days. I prayed in the classroom before, during and after exams. I would pray, "Lord, if you'll just give me the answers to the next five questions, I'll become a missionary."

I prayed particularly hard before algebra exams. I was a regular Billy Graham before an algebra exam.

I also prayed before I opened my report cards. I believed in miracles, and I was absolutely convinced that if the Lord could part the waters of the Red Sea, He could certainly change by biology grade from a "D" to a "B."

When I was in high school, I prayed every day while I walked to class. I had to walk past the school's smoking area, which was the hangout for a group of my fellow classmates who were voted "most likely to someday spend time in a federal institution." As I walked past the smoking area, I would pray, "Yea, though I walk through the valley of the smoking area, I will fear no evil. Switchblades, yes; evil, no."

And yes, I prayed during my high school graduation ceremonies. I thanked the Lord that I had survived the smoking area and the algebra exams. I thanked Him for pulling off yet another series of miracles of Old Testament proportions, changing several grades on my report card. And I thanked Him for forgetting all about my hasty promise to become a missionary. I'm not sure He has ever forgiven me for becoming a lawyer.

If I want my kids to pray in school, I guess I'll just have to send them to Vacation Bible School. In the public schools, they haven't got a prayer.

Fun With Dick And Jane
And Politicians

See the politicians. See the politicians run. The politicians are always running for office. Run, politicians, run!

Hear the politicians make promises. The politicians always make promises while they run. They promise everything to everyone, and (here's the good part) they promise that it will cost the voters absolutely nothing. Run, politicians, run!

See the voters. See the voters clap and cheer for the politicians who promise them everything at absolutely no cost.

See the children. See the children go to school at the old schoolhouse. It is the same schoolhouse where their parents (Dick and Jane) went to school long ago.

See the old schoolhouse. It is in the same condition it was when Dick and Jane went to school there back when the politicians were Truman and Eisenhower. The schoolhouse is hot, crowded and falling apart.

See the politicians. See the politicians promise the children that they will build a new schoolhouse and (here's the good part) it will cost the voters absolutely nothing! Hooray! Run, politicians, run!

See the recession. The recession is bad. The recession is so bad that the politicians do not have the money to build the new schoolhouse.

See the recession get worse. See the recession get so bad that not only do the politicians lack the money to build the new schoolhouse, but they cannot even keep open the old schoolhouse that is all about to fall apart anyway.

See the children. They are sad. See the children's parents. They are mad. They are mad at the politicians because the politicians have not yet built the new schoolhouse that they promised.

"Where is the new schoolhouse?" the parents ask the politicians.

The politicians answer, "Well, it seems we do not have the money for the new schoolhouse."

"But, wait a minute!" cry the parents. "You promised us something for nothing! How can you now tell us you do not have the money for the new schoolhouse?"

See the teacher. She is very sad. She is sad because, thanks to the politicians, she had very little to begin with, and now it is going to get even worse.

See the teacher try to teach the children math in the old schoolhouse. The teacher asks the students, "If you had five apples and I took five apples from you, how many apples would you have?"

"None," answer the children, who, after all, are very smart.

"Suppose," the teacher continues, "you had five apples and

I promised to give you 10 apples but took away your five apples and didn't give you any more. How many apples would you have?"

"None," reply the children, who aren't Japanese but still have a lot of potential.

See the politicians. See the politicians promise the children and their parents that everything is going to be OK. The politicians say: "We're working real hard on this, and we promise you that we'll figure out a way to build the new schoolhouse, and it will cost you absolutely nothing."

The politicians need a math lesson.

Run, politicians, run.

Protect Your Children From Mr. Ed

A federal judge in East Tennessee has ruled that the county public-school system violated the civil rights of certain school children by requiring them to read textbooks that offended the kids' religious beliefs. At issue was something called the Holt, Rhinehart and Winston Basic Reading Series. According to the plaintiffs, the textbooks in this series were written by "secular humanists" who advocated "the views of a feminist, a humanist, a pacifist . . . a vegetarian, or an advocate of one-world government."

One can just imagine the Holt Rhinehart offices (probably in New York City, next to the United Nations Building) full of women authors who munch cauliflower and sing *Give Peace a Chance* while they write books such as *Ronald McDonald Eats a Veggie Burger.*

Well the judge ruled for the plaintiffs, and unless some humanist appellate judges reverse the decision, Tennessee school children will soon have a theological trump card to play on their teachers. Yes, sweet little old Miss Landers (B.A., George Peabody College, 1947) will assign Beaver and his classmates to read Silas Marner. Faster than you can say "book report," Lumpy Rutherford's lawyer will slap her with a temporary restraining order.

Frankly, this decision comes twenty years too late for me. Had it been issued in say, 1967, when I was in the ninth grade, I guarantee you I would have told my parents that Algebra offended my basic religious beliefs. I wouldn't have stopped there. History? Mom, they make us read about non-believers! Latin? Dad, it's the language of a bunch of pagans? Physics? That teacher is trying to destroy everything I learned in Vacation Bible School last summer. Biology? I don't think the Lord wants me to cut open a dead frog.

Yessireebob, I would have said, "Let's hire a Christian lawyer (if we can find one), get an affidavit from a preacher, and let's sue the humanists!"

Well, I would have tried, but it wouldn't have worked. Despite the fact that my father was (and is) a Baptist minister, and my mother led the Women's Missionary Union, they would have told me to shut up, go back to class, and try to learn something. They would have taken me back to church on Wednesday nights and Sundays, innocent of the fact that my public-school teachers were secretly undermining my religious beliefs.

To show you just how naive my parents were, they let me watch the *Mr. Ed* television show, which along with *My Mother the Car*, was my favorite TV show. Only in the 1980s have we learned from certain cable-television evangelists that if we had played the *Mr. Ed* theme song backwards, we would have heard the talking humanist horse singing the praises of Satan. ("Well, Wil-bur, let's eat some vegetables!")

My parents and I never played the *Mr. Ed* theme song backwards. Nevertheless, we know now that as we listened to the song 30 years ago, the subliminal satanic message came through. It came right from the source, of course, of course.

My Mother the Car was probably possessed too. Or maybe she was repossessed.

No doubt about it, my parents were strange. They never sued a teacher for spanking me. They never called my principal and demanded equal time for the Genesis account of creation. They never felt that what I was learning in school was a threat to what I was learning in church. I guess they had the silly notion that if some secular humanist ever challenged our faith, our faith would be strong enough to meet the challenge.

They didn't know that Mr. Ed, the talking horse, and Miss Landers, the talking English teacher, were dangerous.

I guess my folks weren't as smart as parents are today.

Section VI

It's A Part Of This Complete Breakfast!

Start Your Day With Captain Krispies Sugar-Coated Chocolate Chewies!

Every Saturday morning my children do two things. First, they watch violent cartoon programs such as the Road Runner Show.

Second, while watching the violent cartoon shows, they eat at least 27 consecutive bowls of sugar-covered cereal.

Poor Wile E. Coyote straps on his Acme Rocket Sled in a desperate attempt to catch Road Runner. And then, as the ill-fated Wile E. blasts himself over the side of a cliff, my kids gulp down another bowl of Captain Krispie Sugar Flakes.

Then, while Road Runner pushes a boulder over the cliff to score a direct hit on the already-seriously-wounded Wile E. Coyote, my boys dig in to another bowl of Honey Bunny Sugar Crunchies!

This is no coincidence. It's all a part of a nutritional conspiracy between network cartoon show producers, cereal manufacturers, and your dentist.

Most Saturday morning cartoon shows are sponsored by cereal companies. (In fact, to my knowledge, the Acme Rocket Sled Company does not sponsor a single cartoon show.)

Consequently, several times each hour, Wile E. Coyote is given a very short reprieve so that the cereal companies can air commercials urging kids to eat a hearty breakfast featuring enough sugar to sweeten a cup of coffee the size of Lake Michigan.

If you've seen one commercial for children's cereal, you've seen them all. Captain Krispie or Sir Sugarlot or some other animated spokesperson for the cereal industry appears on the screen and dances around in an effort to persuade the kiddies to urge mom and dad to buy them the cereal. Then at the end of the commercial, the viewer is shown a nice breakfast of eggs, bacon, toast, pancakes, yogurt, fruit, milk, juice, and a bowl of the cereal being advertised. An announcer then says, "Captain Krispies' Crunchies are a part of this complete breakfast!" (This is like saying that this column is part of a complete newspaper.)

Well, no problem with truth in advertising here. In fact, they could substitute a dead muskrat for the bowl of cereal and truthfully say, "This dead muskrat is a part of this complete breakfast."

Well, I guess there's really no harm in all this. After all, 40 years ago I spent my Saturday mornings watching Tony the Tiger urge me to have another bowl of Sugar-Frosted Flakes while I watched Pixie and Dixie stick Mr. Jenks' tail into an electrical outlet. And then, Roy Rogers and Trigger would urge me to eat a bowl of Cowboy Sugar Krunchies while I watched

Bugs Bunny push an anvil on top of Yosemite Sam.

I guess I wasn't harmed by any of this.

While I've had my share of cavities along the way, I have never once felt the urge to take a ride on an Acme Rocket Sled or to drop an anvil or push a boulder on top of one of my co-workers.

However, it does make you wonder what poor Wile E. Coyote eats for breakfast.

Halloween Is A Conspiracy Of The American Dental Association

Next Tuesday night is Halloween, that special annual night when neighborhoods across America are terrorized by millions of little yard apes dressed like ghosts and goblins. These little terrorists appear on our front porches, ring our doorbells, and demand that we give them candy bars.

I don't mean to sound like the Grinch Who Stole Halloween, but I'm convinced that this annual event is the result of a conspiracy by the American Dental Association.

One night each October every kid in America under the age of 18 is given enough cavity-filled treats to support every dentist in America for an entire year.

I will be personally responsible for two of the little yard apes who will be terrorizing my neighborhood next Tuesday night.

For the past few weeks, Wally and Beaver Haltom have been preparing for Halloween in much the same manner that the United States Marines prepare for an amphibious landing. The boys have charted a course through our neighborhood designed to maximize the recovery of Snickers, Milky Ways, Milk Duds, and GooGoo Clusters.

Based on past Halloweens and highly sophisticated intelligence operations, the boys know exactly which neighbors pass out what sort of treats on Halloween night. For example, they know that Mrs. Nichols around the corner is a health nut who enjoys a holistic multi-grain vegetarian lifestyle. Consequently on Halloween night, she passes out carrot sticks and tofu bars.

She must be avoided at all costs.

On the other hand, the boys know that Dr. Jones up the street is a chain-smoking retired physician who has a cholesterol count of over 400. On Halloween night, he'll be passing out Snickers bars dipped in egg yolk. If we don't watch him carefully, he'll also pass out cigarettes.

The boys plan on hitting his house at least three times.

The boys have also spent several hours selecting their costumes. They both want to dress in the most terrorizing costume imaginable. Accordingly, after giving the matter due consideration, they decided to dress as F. Lee Bailey and Johnnie Cochran.

My wife and I vetoed these costumes since we didn't want to create a wholesale panic throughout the neighborhood.

The boys then suggested they go trick-or-treating dressed as Bill Clinton and Newt Gingrich. Once again, my wife and I had to tell the boys that it was one thing to dress up in scary outfits, but it was another to cause our neighbors to have heart attacks.

Finally, both boys decided to go trick-or-treating dressed as

Ross Perot. It will still be a pretty scary sight, but at least their ears will be funny.

I'm thinking about joining the boys on Halloween night for a little trick-or-treating myself. I'd love to snarf down a couple of GooGoo Clusters, and I've already picked out a pretty scary costume of my own. I'm going to go dressed as an auditor for the Internal Revenue Service.

Munching Goobers And Raisinettes At The Mall Cinema

When it comes to movies, my wife and I are no Siskel and Ebert.

We know very little about the films that win the Academy Awards. Until recently, my wife thought that *Driving Miss Daisy* was an animated feature about Donald Duck's girlfriend. As for me, well, let's just say I didn't know *My Left Foot* from my right one.

The fact of the matter is we rarely see a film made for grown-ups. But when it comes to kids' flicks, well, move over, Roger and Gene, and make way for the experts!

At least once a month, my wife and I take our boys to the mall cinema. There, after buying enough popcorn and Raisinettes to feed an army battalion, we take our seats and enjoy an outstanding motion picture, such as *The Little Mermaid* or *Nightmare on Sesame Street*.

We've enjoyed some very tender family moments together as we munched on buttered popcorn. We cried together as we watched Bambi's mother get harvested. We laughed together as we watched the Muppets take Manhattan. And as the great American philosopher Frank Sinatra has said, if the Muppets can make it there, they can make it anywhere.

We cheered together as we watched those immortal tortoises, the Teenage Mutant Ninja Turtles, fight for truth, justice and pepperoni pizzas. Their film can give us all hope that even in the post-Chernobyl world, some good things may come from radiation. Specifically, it may cause household pets to grow to be giant crime-fighters.

We've also sat through some films that were so bad that even Wally and Beaver gave them two thumbs down. For example, we were recently subjected to a film called *Ernest Goes to Jail*. Talk about cruel and unusual punishment. All I can say is that after watching this film, we look forward to a sequel titled *Ernest Gets the Death Penalty*.

I must admit that my wife and I get a little weary of watching movies that feature mice or singing crickets in the leading roles. But kids' flicks have a lot of advantages over films for grown-ups. With the exception of Road Runner cartoons, kids' films are never violent. You'll never hear Jiminy Cricket say something like, "Go ahead. Make my day!"

Most important, kids' flicks always have a happy ending. The good mice always win.

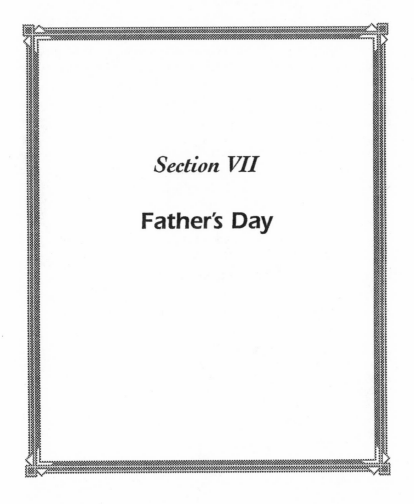

Section VII

Father's Day

What Daddy Wants
For Father's Day

According to the Ronald Reagan Institute for Reliable Statistics, 99 percent of America's daddies get the same present every Father's Day, specifically, either a new tie or a bottle of after shave.

Given my impeccable daddy credentials, I feel highly qualified to serve as a spokesperson on behalf of the daddies of America. After all, Ozzie Nelson, Danny Thomas, and Hugh Beaumont are all dead. Somebody's got to step up to the bully pulpit of Fatherhood and speak up, and it might as well be me.

Therefore, on behalf of the daddies of America, let me make this perfectly clear: We daddies are sick and tired of getting the same old Father's Day gifts year after year after year. Specifically, we don't need or want any of the following items:

- Ties
- After shave
- Weed-eaters
- One of those goofy "Father's Day books" such as *A Father's Guide to Wisdom* ("Number 47: Learn to drive a stick shift." "Number 163: Watch a sunrise at least once

a year." "Number 512: Never take investment advice from either your brother-in-law or an airline pilot." "Number 613: Never vote for a presidential candidate who was once the governor of a southern state.")

• Any product advertised on late night TV, i.e. the Ronco Home Barber, The Popeil Pocket Fisherman, a gift certificate from The Legal Clinic of J. Cheaver Loophole, etc.

I don't mean to sound ungrateful, but let me assure you that there is not one daddy in America who needs a new tie. If you don't believe me, check it out yourself. Tonight, while daddy is on the sofa watching *Wheel of Fortune*, inspect his tie rack. You'll find hundreds of ties of all colors, shapes, and sizes, dating back to the Truman administration. We dads need a new tie like Bill Clinton needs a gift certificate to Dunkin Donuts.

Let me also assure you that we don't need another bottle of after shave or cologne. If you look in daddy's shaving kit, you'll find that same unopened bottle you gave him for Father's Day in 1982. Also, we aren't interested in one of those new fragrances such as Calvin Klein's Obsessive Compulsive Neurotic Personality.

So what do we daddies want for Father's Day? Well, here is a short wish list of gifts that are guaranteed to bring a smile to any dad's face:

• A voice-activated remote control channel changer ("ESPN! Now!")

- A combination golf cart-riding lawn mower-recliner chair.
- A videotape collection of every film made by the Three Stooges (Only we daddies appreciate the Stooges' sophisticated, dry sense of humor).
- A year-long pass to Earl's Bowl-A-Rama.
- A subscription to a daily newspaper that has no coverage whatsoever of the O.J. Simpson trial.
- A custom built minivan featuring a soundproof driver's compartment.
- An automatic, self-cleaning child.
- An all-expense paid trip to Disney World . . . for the wife and kids.

So what are you waiting for? Take that tie back to the men's store at the mall and exchange it for something daddy really wants, such as a pair of fur-lined wing tips.

Remembering Grandaddy When I Play Cow Pasture Pool

My late grandfather called golf "cow pasture pool." He made fun of city fellers who spent their weekends knocking a little white ball around a well-mowed pasture.

Grandaddy grew up in a place called Deanburg, Tennessee, an urban center that had several cow pastures but not one golf course.

Grandaddy hated golf for two reasons. First, he regarded it as a "Republican game" that was played by rich folks. You see, Grandaddy was a life-long "yeller-dawg Democrat" who blamed Republicans for the Civil War, Reconstruction, the Depression, and just about any other bad thing that ever happened to folks in Deanburg, Tennessee. In fact, Grandaddy was such a "yeller-dawg Democrat" that he actually voted for George McGovern for president in 1972. Fortunately, Grandaddy didn't live to see Michael Dukakis.

Whenever my Grandfather saw a picture of President Eisenhower playing golf, it made his yeller-dawg Democrat blood boil. He would grumble, "There's that Republican playing cow pasture pool. You never see Harry Truman wasting his time in a cow pasture."

Second, my Grandaddy hated golf because he believed that

it had caused the creation of Daylight Savings Time.

Like most folks in Deanburg, Tennessee, my Grandfather got up when the sun came up and went to bed when it got dark. He thought the idea of moving your clock forward each spring to get another hour of sunlight was ridiculous. He once told me, "Daylight Savings Time is like cutting off the top part of my blanket and sewing it to the bottom of my blanket so that I can have a longer blanket. That's ridiculous."

Grandaddy knew exactly who to blame for Daylight Savings Time. "It was invented by those city guys who play cow pasture pool," he explained. "They got the legislature to pass a law making us change the clocks in the summertime so that they can play golf after work when it is still daylight but is really supposed to be night."

No doubt about it, Grandaddy had no use for Republican city slickers who forced everybody to move their clocks forward one hour each spring so that they could spend their evenings playing cow pasture pool.

Grandaddy died in 1973. I wish he had lived one more year so that he could have watched Nixon resign. That would have warmed Grandaddy's yeller-dawg Democrat heart since Nixon was both a Republican and a golfer, and therefore deserved to be impeached.

I miss my Grandaddy, and I think about him often. I think about him each year on the first Sunday in April when I advance my clock one hour for Daylight Savings Time.

I think about him every time I'm in the voting booth and I'm about to pull the Republican lever.

I think about him whenever I see Bill Clinton on TV playing that Republican game, golf.

But above all, I think about him on these bright, sun-lit summer evenings when I knock the little white ball down a well-mowed city cow pasture.

I Was A Middle-Class Daddy When Being A Middle-Class Daddy Wasn't Cool

A few years ago, Barbara Mandrell recorded a song entitled, *I Was Country When Country Wasn't Cool.* In the song, Barbara (who should not be confused with either Hillary Clinton or Tammy Wynette) warbled about how she had always worn boots and blue jeans and eaten Goo Goo Clusters while riding around in a pickup truck. And then one day (Barbara sang), sophisticated folks in New York and Hollywood decided that the cool thing was to wear boots and blue jeans and eat Goo Goo Clusters while riding around in a pickup truck.

Well, I have decided I am going to record a song entitled *I Was a Middle-Class Daddy When Being a Middle-Class Daddy Wasn't Cool.*

For years, I have been a hopeless square. I've stayed at home, ordered pizza, played with my kids, and watched ESPN's Jackpot Bowling while my really cool friends were out eating sushi and drinking Perrier at fern bars.

But incredibly, my lifestyle has now become cool. At least that's what the really sophisticated folks in cool places such as

New York and Hollywood are saying.

In New York, there was an official announcement recently that the cool thing to do in the 1990s is "to be normal and have a regular life." This announcement came from a woman with the unlikely name of Faith Popcorn. (Sounds like a snack food for preachers.) Ms. Popcorn is a "trendologist." That is to say, she is an expert in lifestyles and trends, and people actually pay her money for advice on what is cool.

Now if a person has so much money that he or she can consult with a "trendologist" to find out what is cool, that person definitely has too much money. But that's beside the point.

The point is that Ms. Popcorn has announced that the Yuppie lifestyle is over. The era of BMWs, trips to Club Med, and endless gulping of French mineral water has come to an end. Ms. Popcorn says that the new trend is something called "cocooning." This is trendologists' lingo for staying at home with the kids and watching TV.

Meanwhile, on the other side of the continent, those really cool folks in Hollywood are busy cranking out films that sing the praises of family values. Nominees for next year's Oscar for Best Picture will probably be *Indiana Jones Attends a PTA Meeting* and *Rambo Drives Car Pool*.

Meanwhile, fashion designers in New York are discussing the new trend of "downscaling." This is trendologists' lingo for buying your clothes at J.C. Penney's and driving a Buick, rather than buying Italian suits at a thousand dollars a pop and cruising around town in a stretch limo. It's move over, Donald Trump and Nancy Reagan! Make way for Barbara Bush and, well, me.

And so, after over 40 years of being a hopeless square, I have become a stylish man for the '90s. I have the right clothes (non-designer blue jeans from Sears), the right car (a non-Japanese minivan), and I eat really cool food (meatloaf, Big Macs, a side order of fries, and of course, Goo Goo Clusters.)

As Barbara Mandrell would put it, I was downscaling and cocooning when downscaling and cocooning weren't cool.

When I Win The Publisher's Clearinghouse Sweepstakes I'm Going To Live Like Ozzie Nelson

Move over, Murphy Brown! Ward and June Cleaver appear to be making a comeback.

According to a report recently issued by the United States Census Bureau, the number of two-parent households is on the rise. America now has over 25 million married couples with children. In fact, the number of married couples with kids has increased by more than a half million over the past five years.

Somewhere Danny Quayle must be smiling.

I'm a lucky man. I'm a daddy in one of the 25 million mom-and-dad-and-the-kids households.

But we Cleavers of the '90s bear little resemblance to Wally and Beaver's mom and dad. For example, my wife never wears pearls, and I never walk around the house wearing a tie, a shirt, and an Ozzie Nelson-style golf sweater. I don't dare dress that way around the house. I have a five-month old daughter whose idea of a good time is to spit up on her daddy.

I can't recall a single episode of *Leave It To Beaver* in which Wally or the Beav barfed on Ward. Nevertheless, whenever I'm wearing a dark suit, my five-month old daughter sees this as an opportunity to engage in spit-up target practice.

I keep expecting Eddie Haskell to walk in my house at breakfast one morning and say, "That's a beautiful blue suit you're wearing, Mr. Haltom. Too bad you have baby barf all over your shoulder."

My wife and I generally wear t-shirts and blue jeans around the house. Now that I think about it, I can't recall a single episode of *Leave It To Beaver* in which June Cleaver was wearing a t-shirt and blue jeans. I'm not quite sure pearls and high-heeled shoes go with t-shirts and blue jeans anyway.

But perhaps the biggest difference between the Ward and June Cleavers of the '90s and the Cleavers of the '50s is that these days, Ward and June both go to the office.

In the 1950s, only Daddy went to the office. In fact, the only successful dad in the 1950s who did not go to the office every day was Ozzie Nelson. To this day, I haven't the slightest idea what Ozzie Nelson did for a living. I don't know how he could afford all those golf sweaters. He must have won the grand prize in the Publisher's Clearinghouse Sweepstakes.

These days, June is not a homebody. She's become June Rodham Cleaver, Esquire, or June Barbara Billingsley-Cleaver, corporate executive.

Moreover, unlike Ward, I do not go directly to my office every day. I begin the day as a chauffeur, driving car-pool for the Wallys and Beavers of the 1990s. Again, I can't recall a single episode of *Leave It To Beaver* in which Ward started the day by driving Lumpy Rutherford, Eddie Haskell, and Wally and Beaver to school.

But despite the differences between the Cleavers of the '50s and the Cleavers of the '90s, traditional two-parent households appear to be making a comeback. I feel fortunate to be a part of this trend. However, I have to admit I'd much rather be like Ozzie Nelson than Ward Cleaver. If I ever win the grand prize in the Publisher's Clearinghouse Sweepstakes, I'm going to spend every day at home walking around in my golf sweater.

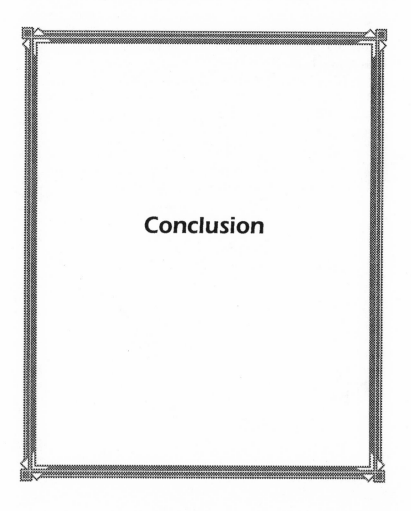

Conclusion

A Tribute To The
Finest Dad I Ever Met

I'm 43 years old. I have a wife, three kids, a dog, a cat, a mini-van, and an adjustable rate mortgage. Nevertheless, I still think of myself as someone who has just borrowed the car keys from Dad.

You see, even though I am now a middle-aged daddy and, technically speaking, an official "grown-up," I will always be in awe of my dad and the other dads of his generation.

My daddy is a remarkable man and a member of an equal-ly-remarkable generation. Dad was born in the booming metropolis of Bemis, Tennessee in 1924. He grew up during the Depression in a home owned by the mill where my grandparents worked.

I guess my grandparents were a "two career family." But they didn't both work at the Bemis Mill for glamour. They did it to make ends meet.

Dad was a senior in high school on December 7, 1941 when the news came that the Japanese had bombed Pearl Harbor.

After graduating from high school, Dad joined the Navy, and Uncle Sam eventually sent him to the South Pacific.

In late 1945, having literally saved civilization, my dad and other members of his generation came home. Dad went back to school on the G.I. Bill, and in 1948, he became the first member of his family to graduate from college.

Dad moved to Memphis and went to work as an auditor for the E.L. Bruce Company. There he found more than a job. He met and fell in love with my Mamma. After a five-month courtship, she asked him to marry her, and he said yes.

Mamma and Dad bought a little two-bedroom suburban house. The house was about 1200 square feet big, but for a boy from Bemis who grew up during the Depression, it was a mansion.

But the mansion got a little crowded on a hot summer day in 1952 when Mamma and Dad brought me home from Methodist Hospital.

For the past 43 years, my dad has always been there for me. He was there for me when I first learned to crawl and then walk and then run.

He was there for me when I first learned to ride a two-wheel bike.

He was there for me when I broke my arm while playing Tarzan, swinging out of a tree in the neighbor's back yard.

He was there for me during my terrible Little League baseball career as a short stop for the Dellwood Baptist Cardinals. (I was the Marv Thornberry of the Dellwood Baptist Cardinals.)

He was there for me when I sat in the Malco Theater in downtown Memphis and watched *Old Yeller*. He consoled me when I cried after Old Yeller died.

He was there for me on my first day of school in 1958. Dad walked me to my classroom and introduced himself to my first grade teacher, Mrs. Oswald. The school was safe and clean, and Dad and I did not have to walk through metal detectors as we went through the schoolhouse doors.

My dad was there for me on a glorious summer day in 1959 when he took me to Sportsmen's Park in St. Louis to see the St. Louis Cardinals play the Milwaukee Braves. We saw Henry Aaron and Stan Musial and a pitcher named Ernie Broglio who would later be traded to the Cubs for Lou Brock.

Dad was there for me every morning at breakfast, sitting beside me in his grey flannel suit and his black wingtips which are of course, the official shoes of old-fashioned daddies.

Dad was with me every night at dinner, asking me how my day had gone and whether I was minding Mrs. Oswald.

Dad was there for me for birthday parties and Christmas mornings, to make sure I got my Davy Crockett coonskin cap or a hoola hoop or a pogo stick.

Dad was there for me when I competed in Pinewood Derby races, spelling bees, oratorical contests, and basketball games during my brief career as a four foot tall power forward.

. . . And Dad was with me on a cold January day in 1966 when my mother went to heaven.

Dad was also with me on April 21, 1985, the day I became a daddy and he became a grandpa.

I will never forget what my dad said as he held his first grandson in his arms. He looked at me and said, "Bill, you're a rich man."

Dad, of course, was right. I am blessed and rich not only because I have children of my own, but because I have an old-fashioned caring dad who survived a Depression, won a World War, married his sweetheart, and tried to teach a little boy what it means to be a man.

And if I ever grow up, I want to be just like him.

About The Author

Bill Haltom is a humor columnist for the *Naples Daily News*. His columns are also carried by the Scripps Howard News Service and are published in numerous other newspapers, journals and magazines.

Bill is married to Claudia Swafford Haltom, a Juvenile Court Referee Judge in Memphis. He and Claudia have two sons who, contrary to popular belief, are not named Wally and Beaver. They are Will, age 10, and Ken, age 7.

Bill and Claudia are also the proud parents of a gender-correct baby, Margaret Grace.